HOW TO
GET INTO DEBT

THE *Self-Hurt* SERIES

KNOCK
KNOCK.
VENICE, CALIFORNIA

Published by
Knock Knock
1633 Electric Avenue
Venice, CA 90291
www.knockknock.biz

Illustrated by Mark Weber

ISBN: 978-160106042-6
UPC: 825703-50104-9

CONTENTS

CHAPTER 1
INTRODUCTION:
FOR YOURSELF, FOR YOUR NATION

DEBT IS FUN. SOME PEOPLE CLAIM it's a curse, others spend sleepless nights worrying about how much they owe. For those who incur debt deliberately and recklessly, however, debt brings sheer, unadulterated glee. You can't get into debt without spending more money than you make, and what's more fun than spending money, especially if you don't have to earn it? That's right—nothing.

The trick to debt success is twofold: one, understanding that stress over debt is neurotic, counterproductive, and anti-American; and two, tackling debt accrual with a passion for spending. Merely dipping your toe in the water, only to pull back with an out-dated, misplaced sense of guilt is for debt novices and chumps. It's true that decades ago debt was discouraged, and the only occasion upon which most people sought bank credit was for the purchase of their home. The credit card as we currently know it was only introduced in 1950! Most new technologies are misused, underemployed, and disparaged as the downfall of civiliza-tion in their first years of existence, and credit—another word for means by which to amass debt—is one of them. No doubt you consider yourself modern in many ways; this book will help bring you into the twenty-first century with debt.

Perhaps you've had trouble getting into debt before. Maybe you're already in debt, but would like to delve more deeply. Or it's entirely possible that you're in debt up to your eyeballs and just want to celebrate your capabilities by seeing yourself reflected in the pages of this book. Whatever your motivation, *How to Get into Debt* will teach you how to embrace and luxuriate in debt. We'll help you turn any negatives you may previously have heard or experienced into positives. We'll guide you step by step into making the most of your debt to live the lifestyle you *deserve*. Whether you want to winter in the Caribbean and summer in the Hamptons or build an 8-bedroom, 11-bath McMansion and drive Escalades in three different colors, *How to Get into Debt* will make all your dreams come true. You'll learn:

- Why spending is patriotic.

- Why shame is no longer shameful.

- What your debt style is: country lane or autobahn.

- How to spot the evils of IRAs, Keoghs, and savings accounts, not to mention checks and debit cards.

- Whether you should have a premium credit card or an affinity credit card (hint: many of both!).

- How to turn wants into needs in order to jack up your monthly nut.

- How to shop and spend like the wife of a despot.

- When and how to manage your debt.

The Debt Revolution

Sadly, in any store and restaurant you can still find financial dinosaurs who pay their bills in full—including some who even use coupons. These outdated and unhappy

> ## Words Disbursed
>
> "Speak not of my debts, unless you mean to pay them."
>
> —George Herbert

individuals don't understand that the world is passing them by. They're stuck in their ways and probably wouldn't even own a car or computer if they didn't have to commute to work and check their bank balance. Pity them, for they are a dying breed. Given the speed of change in our contemporary world, one day soon they will no longer be around, and the newer generation will take their place. Born with a credit card in their mouths and with no firsthand experience of cash, future citizens of the world will look upon even this book as archaic. "Why," they will ask, "would anyone have doubted debt?"

With any paradigm shift, however, there are those who are left behind and those who come after. Those in the middle—forward-thinking individuals such as yourself—are perched on the vanguard of change. You are to be commended for your courage. The fact that you may still have doubts and questions in no way mitigates this bravery; rather, it shows that you are a thoughtful, intelligent person who wants to implement a major life change with eyes wide open. The goal of *How to Get into Debt* is not only to give you the tools of debt, it's to reassure you that you've made the right decision.

Macrocosmic Benefits of Debt

In economics, the terms "macrocosmic" and "microcosmic" are bandied about, with *macro-* referring to the economy overall, and *micro-* referring to the economics of individual businesses. In *How to Get into Debt*, *micro-* refers to the impact of debt on you as an individual. Though the joy of personal debt is reason enough to embark on this lifestyle, you'll be happy to know that there are larger, macrocosmic reasons why you've made the right choice.

Debt Is Patriotic

Never was our civic duty more pronounced than after the tragic events of September 11, 2001. In addressing airline employees at O'Hare International Airport, President George W. Bush told the country to "Get down to Disney World in Florida. Take your families and enjoy life, the way we want it to be enjoyed." The next day, Prime Minister Tony Blair of the United Kingdom held a news conference to tell the world "to shop" to keep economies from going into recession. Mayor Rudolph Giuliani called New Yorkers "the best shoppers in the world" and exhorted them to return to restaurants, the theater, and stores.

In December 2006, well into the second Iraq War, President Bush reiterated his earlier inspiring comments. He advised the American people that their role at home was "keeping our economy going." To that end, stated President Bush, "I encourage you all to go shopping more."

Spending money keeps the economy going. You will notice that none of these world leaders said to go shopping "only if you have money in the bank" or "only if your spending doesn't

Trillion Means 12 Zeros!

In the last 50 years, the total national debt of the United States has grown from $257 billion to over $8.8 trillion as of 2007. Per citizen, that works out to be over $29,000! Between October 2006 and June 2007, the increase in national debt averaged $1.3 billion per day. How could that be interpreted as anything other than a pro-debt stance from government?

exceed your income." They didn't tell us to use cash or checks rather than credit cards. They just told us to shop, go on vacations, and enjoy life—"the way we want it to be enjoyed."

Easy consumer credit is as American as apple pie—indeed, one of the ways we can buy apple pie. We invented credit, we give credit, we take credit. Spending is not only the great American pastime, it's the American Dream.

Consumer spending has historically comprised two-thirds of gross domestic purchases. If we stop spending, our economy will die.

Fortunately, here in the New World (and increasingly in the rest of the world), money practically grows on the trees we cut down to build our new homes. Credit card companies throw themselves at the American consumer, car loans can be obtained without a credit history, and houses can be purchased with no money down. The right to credit and debt is practically the twenty-eighth amendment of the Constitution, our birthright as Americans!

The United States government also carries debt—almost $9 trillion as of 2007. Our leaders wouldn't do this unless they intended for us to do the same. When the government borrows money to spend on roads, schools, and defense, it improves our infrastructure, employs Americans, and helps the economy grow.

The beauty of all this debt is that no one will ever have to pay for it. We will leave our children a purple mountain's majesty of debt, which our children will then pass on to their children, and so on. The noble tradition of debt we are starting will become part of the American legacy, like grandma's recipe for cranberry stuffing.

Debt Is the Global Future

As with everything worthwhile (for example, fast food), the United States is fueling a global debt revolution.

The Spendthrift's Insula

If you're having trouble getting over the hump of spending big bucks, don't feel bad—your brain chemistry might be to blame. Scientists at Carnegie Mellon have discovered that an overactive insula (an area in the brain associated with discomfort) and underactive nucleus accumbens (an area associated with the anticipation of pleasure) can render a shopper biologically reluctant to hand over her cash. While some lucky debt embracers feel joy when they spend, others experience sensations of extreme displeasure at the moment of purchase.

To get around this unfortunate physiological flaw, look for opportunities to spend large sums of money all at once that will yield a satisfying return over time. Try a caviar-of-the-month club, participate in a timeshare, or buy a year's worth of luxury spa packages. The key is ripping off the spending Band-Aid with one quick tug while assuring maximum returns. Researchers also found that paying with credit cards rather than cash helps dull the insula-induced discomfort, which is perfect for the debt embracer! Opening accounts with online merchants will further distance you from the ache of parting with your money.

American culture is our number-one export, and consumerism is an intrinsic component of what it means to be American today.

In 2006, the average amount of consumer credit debt per capita in the United Kingdom was $6,900, versus the United States at $7,300. However, while American consumer debt grew at only 5 percent from 1993 to 2006, the British managed to grow theirs by 16 percent. They're catching up!

Asian cultures traditionally prioritized saving, but they're getting with the debt program as well. After the financial crisis of 1997, the Korean government encouraged its citizens to use credit cards, and since then, credit card use increased 90 percent per year through 2004. Korea's total outstanding credit card debt escalated from $11 billion in 1999 to $58 billion in 2003. Japan is always keen to jump on the latest American trends, and as of 2002, the Japanese were spending 108 percent of disposable income.

The United States started it, and we're the best. But the word is out, and we're going to have to work to keep our lead. By embracing debt, you are not only an American citizen, you are a citizen of the world.

Corporations Are Debtors

In 1958, Nobel Prize–winning economists Franco Modigliani and Merton Miller published an analysis of corporate debt now known as the "M&M theory." M&M proved that "the value of a firm [is] independent of its capital structure," meaning it didn't matter whether a company was financed with equity or debt. Not to mention that there are also significant tax benefits to debt. It's no wonder that the average American business has a debt-to-equity ratio of 2.58—what they owe is 2.58 times what they own!

Major corporations are advised by the keenest economic minds in the world; the average person would be foolish not to emulate their behaviors. If it makes sense for business, it makes sense for us. Aside from a little speed bump called the Great Depression, this method has inarguably been successful for the American economy.

Nobody Gets It Anyway

Does it make sense to you that you can spend money without having money? If you don't pay it, who will? These are the existential questions of modern times, and there are two answers: "Who cares?" and "Nobody knows." It's all vastly theoretical, and theory doesn't put Whole Foods on the table or Blahniks on your feet. There are those who claim to get it, who claim to grasp where it is the money comes from and goes to, whether it's trillions of dollars of national debt, billions of dollars of corporate debt, millions of dollars of business debt, or thousands of dollars of consumer debt, but they're lying. Nobody gets it, so you shouldn't even try—just know that it works, and if somebody else has to pay for it down the road, so be it. It's more likely, however, that these theoretical people of the future will also find a way to pawn it off (it's a scientifically proven fact that people in the future are always smarter than people in the past), and so the debt will roll through history, snowballing to . . . no effect whatsoever.

Microcosmic Benefits of Debt

Now we get to the fun part—why debt is good for *you*. There are countless ways in which debt will improve your life, in no small part because *life* is now synonymous with *lifestyle*. That's right—the way you live is who you are.

Debt Expands You

In the 1960s, people like Timothy Leary talked about the capability of drugs to expand the mind. That movement, however, had little staying power, because the drug-enhanced experience was imaginary. Spending and buying is real, and with debt, your lifestyle, possessions, real estate, and social circle will truly expand. Leary urged us to "Turn on, tune in, drop out," and some of us did, to little effect. Now the battle cry is "Apply for it, receive it in the mail, spend with it," and the change is real.

Debt Will Make You Happy

We celebrate a raise by running out to buy ourselves a new suit or a new motorcycle for the morning commute. When we fall in love, we buy new lingerie to keep the fire stoked. We reward our kids with a trip to the toy store if they bring home good report cards.

On the other hand, when we experience setbacks and disappointments, we also pull out our wallets—"When the going gets tough, the tough go shopping." After a breakup, there's nothing more therapeutic—"retail therapy"—than a productive excursion to Banana Republic. Everyone has a story about a personal disaster that could only be alleviated by a good credit card workout.

Much of this pleasure is psycho-
logical, but it's also neurochemical:
spending can trigger the brain to

Fictional Money

Need a little inspiration? These films and
television shows will get you in the spending
mood. Whet your appetite by drooling over the
designer clothing, scenic locales, and shiny
luxury items. After your fantasy spending spree,
get out there for the real thing!

Movies

- *Arthur*
- *Clueless*
- *High Society*
- *Metropolitan*
- *Pretty Woman*
- *Richie Rich*
- *The Thomas
  Crown Affair*
- *Trading Places*
- *Wall Street*
- Any James Bond movie

Television Shows

- *Beverly Hills, 90210*
- *Dallas*
- *Dynasty*
- *Entourage*
- *Fresh Prince of Bel-Air*
- *Knots Landing*
- *Lifestyles of the Rich
  and Famous*
- *My Super Sweet 16*
- *The OC*
- *Silver Spoons*

release endorphins and dopamine, the feel-good chemicals that function like opiates in your brain's pleasure centers.

While the boost from buying a new blouse is immediate, spending can also help compensate for an unsatisfying life. It's far easier to fill your life with stuff than it is to meditate, embrace spirituality, exercise, go to therapy, or have a functional family. Those pursuits can take years of practice, and the end result isn't guaranteed. The self-worth that comes from going to the mall and coming home with shopping bags filled with goodies only takes a couple of hours.

Debt Inspires Respect

Forget about keeping up with the Joneses—pull ahead of them! With debt, you can go beyond mere social acceptance to attain respect in your community. Having great stuff equals status. No matter where you live, it's human nature to want to belong and be a part of the in-crowd. In high school, we need the right pair of jeans. In college, it's the right car. In adulthood, the right house, and in retirement, a great condo decorated in the right pastels.

One of the basic human needs is belonging; it's desperately important to feel like you're a part of something. With debt, you'll develop a full social calendar, schedule playdates for your kids, and avoid embarrassment at the tennis club when you valet with the other SUVs. Debt is the universal equalizer—whether you're a lawyer

> **Debtor's Dictionary**
>
> ***two commas***: One million dollars. "Three commas," one billion dollars. "To have two commas," to be a millionaire.
>
> ***decimal dust***: An amount of money so small that it's not even worth thinking about.

or a convenience-store clerk, you can borrow money to live the high life.

Long Live Debt

Whether you do it for your country or for yourself, debt will fulfill you in ways you never dreamed possible. And in addition to the emotional expansion you're about to experience, you'll have lots of great stuff! What good is having a plasma-screen television if you're not happy enough to watch it? Some of you, however, are still battling with the outdated, puritanical voices of your parents and grandparents. Despite your rational understanding that debt is the right choice, you struggle with a deeply instilled sense of shame around debt. In the next chapter, we're going to talk you right through that shame and bring you out on the other end.

CHAPTER 2
THE DEBT EVOLUTION: FROM SHAME TO PRIDE

THANKS TO OUR LEGACY OF FISCAL prudence, many of us still carry the scars of debt prejudice: shame, fear, contempt. Don't feel bad if you yourself are one of these secret debt haters, because you're not alone. It's courageous of you merely to open yourself to learning about debt—leave the rest to us.

We're about to examine the many aspects of resistance around debt, deconstructing the excuses people cite for not getting into debt one by one. By the time you're finished reading this book, all vestiges of your debt denial will be eradicated. You will finally be what you've long imagined: a debt embracer. Of course, you could spend hundreds of hours and thousands of dollars in therapy trying to change your behavior, but we think your dollars are better spent at Saks. In this chapter, we'll show you:

- How history has created debt prejudice.

- Why shame has no place in your repertoire of emotions.

- Why self-denial is actually harmful to your health.

- How to use peer pressure to your advantage.

The Old Debt: Crime, Punishment, Morality

In previous centuries and millennia, debt was not only frowned upon, it was severely punished. The ancient Greeks and Romans condemned debtors to slavery, with the creditor acquiring the debtor as payment and thereafter owning him. From the sixteenth through the nineteenth century, those who owed but could not pay were sent to debtors prison to languish in facilities and conditions far worse than those faced by similarly sentenced criminals. Debtors were sometimes forced to work their debt off in indentured servitude. Other penalties included flogging, ear removal, branding, whipping, wearing publicly identifiable debtor's clothing, and, in some cases, death.

Indebtedness was viewed as a lapse in moral character. Benjamin Franklin loathed debt and uttered such obsolete concepts as "Rather go to bed without dinner than to rise in debt" and "A penny saved is a penny earned." He even contemplated the formation of "The Society of the Free and Easy," in which members would practice the "habit of the virtues . . . industry and frugality, free from debt, which exposes a man to confinement, and a species of slavery to his creditors."

From the Puritans to the Victorians, the United States long equated thrift and self-control with moral virtue. Until the late nineteenth century, credit was extended just to the wealthy, and in the early twentieth century, individuals only used credit to purchase homes. When people wanted to buy something, they waited until they had the money to pay for it, actually *saving* their money to spend their money.

The practice of layaway was common in the twentieth century, whereby a purchase could be made by paying a small amount per month—but only when one finished paying off the purchase was the

Early Consumer Credit: The Car

The early twentieth century marked the first manufacturing of durable goods for the American consumer. As prices fell into affordability for the working person and dealers sought to open broader markets, installment credit—making even payments for a single purchase over a specified period of time—grew in popularity.

Systems of installment credit were embattled and perfected around the sale of cars, particularly by General Motors to triumph over Ford's dominant Model T. Founder Henry Ford was so morally opposed to offering credit that he missed key opportunities to keep his company's lead. The Model T's 1909 offering price, $850, was half the national average, and by 1920, one of every two cars in the world was a Model T. The low price nonetheless comprised one-quarter to one-half of a worker's income, and GM took the opportunity that Ford rejected.

In 1919, GM founded a credit wing to fund its customers' car purchases, launching a boom period in both installment credit and car sales. By 1926, all lower-end car prices had come down to compete with the Model T, two out of every three cars were bought on credit, and Ford's market share had fallen to 36 percent.

item released to bring home. Now stores have replaced their layaway counters with credit card machines. Ads in newspapers and magazines and on television and radio offer "0 percent down!" and "No payments until 2010!" The national savings rate, the average rate of *all* Americans, is negative, meaning all of us are spending more than we earn. Just as we freed ourselves from the bonds of racism and sexism, so too are we now realizing that it's time to leave behind our vilification of debt. Why pull ourselves up by our bootstraps when we've got credit cards?

Spend No Shame

Though the conflation of shame and debt was last valid in the twentieth century, there are still those of you in the third millennium whose minds cannot release the outdated thoughts instilled by your well-intended but misguided elders. These take the form of excuses to stay out of debt, impeding your ability to spend. We'll go through each of the common excuses one by one to help you work through them and move on to productive debt growth.

"I'm ashamed of debt."

People experience shame around characteristics perceived as negative and as being unique to them. "Only I have these thoughts," thinks the person ashamed of sex. "Only I borrow money from my parents," thinks the middle-aged bachelor. Because everyone is in debt, however, and debt keeps the economy going, there is no longer any need to carry debt shame. The Lord's Prayer states "Forgive us our debts, as

---

Debtor's Dictionary

debt porn: Sensationalized stories about individuals who succeed in achieving enormous amounts of debt.

financial porn: Fiction and journalism that celebrates the deals made by businesspeople, especially financiers, money managers, and traders.

---

we also have forgiven our debtors," but when it comes to debt, there's nothing to forgive. When you feel the stab of vestigial debt shame, say to yourself "Debt is *not* shameful. Everybody's in debt, and debt is *normal*," then go out and buy something.

"My parents taught me to save."

When you were a child, your parents probably first gave you a piggy bank then helped you open a savings account with your very own bank-book. Every year after your birthday, they took you to deposit Grandma Berty's $5 birthday check and made you promise to save up for "something special." Your parents were trying to teach you a lesson: if you wanted something you had to save for it, and you should not spend money beyond your means. They were trying to instill in you fiscal responsibility.

But no one's parents are perfect. They were living in a different, and now irrelevant, world. Your memories of that piggy bank won't help you today. Our parents lovingly and selflessly taught us so many things, but that doesn't mean we have to use them. For example, your parents probably taught you to ride a bike, but that doesn't stop you from driving a car. Your job as an adult is to keep your eyes, brain, and heart open to new information, unlearning outdated lessons where necessary. When you linger on the memory of your parents' then-wise words, think to yourself, "Credit is today; thrift is passé."

"If I default, I'll feel guilty."

First of all, never feel guilty. Guilt is an unproductive emotion generated by an internalized disciplinarian. In particular, don't worry about neglecting to pay off your debts. The companies that fail to collect this money can write it off on their taxes and pass it on to other consumers. It's merely a business expense like any other. Even if you don't know it, you're already paying for other people's bad debts, so it's only fair that others should pay for yours. When you receive a bill you can't pay, take a deep breath and put it through the shredder.

"Consumerism and materialism are immoral."

There is a countermovement of debt rejectionists who preach the gospel of antimaterialism. They believe that material goods should not be a substitute for human relationships, that a love of material goods is incompatible with strong moral values, that advertising is a form of brainwashing, that our natural resources are being depleted by overproduction of "unnecessary" products, and that global corporations rule the earth.

Inspirational Magazines

Just charge a few of these subscriptions and let inspiration arrive in your mailbox every month.

- *Architectural Digest*
- *Departures* (only for American Express Platinum or Centurion cardholders)
- *Executive Travel*
- *Food & Wine*
- *Forbes*
- *Golf Digest Index* (only for *Golf Digest* subscribers with annual incomes over $320,000)
- *Luxury SpaFinder*
- The regionals: *Angeleno, AspenPeak, Gotham, Hamptons, Ocean Drive*, etc.
- *Robb Report*
- *Town & Country*
- *Travel + Leisure*
- *W*

What's more, if anybody asks, you can say you're brushing up on your "plutography," a term coined by novelist Tom Wolfe to describe "the great new American vice . . . the graphic depiction of the acts of the rich."

Why would you want to spend time with people like that? If consumerism and materialism were immoral, they wouldn't be so much fun. We are entitled to the "pursuit of happiness." If that happiness comes in the form of a BMW, who are we to judge?

"Self-denial is good for me."

By definition, self-denial is denying your very *self*. How could that be good? In *Civilization and Its Discontents*, Sigmund Freud wrote that self-denial and renunciation of instincts causes repression and chronic mental illness. Today, psychologists assert that self-denial is detrimental to emotional and physical health, resulting in bitterness, depression, and alienation. To practice self-denial is to forgo satisfying your desires and worldly pleasures in an age governed by self-fulfillment and self-enjoyment. Are you any less virtuous because you don't mortify your own flesh, subjecting it to flogging and puncturing? Of course not, and neither does self-deprivation make you a better person.

"My past efforts to get into debt didn't work."

You're not alone. There are many of us who go shopping but not enough, who borrow money but pay it back promptly, who buy used cars outright, who take out mortgages but pay their credit cards off every month. Perhaps your progress has been hampered by worries about how much money you owe, by trouble sleeping, or by cold sweats.

If you've started a get-into-debt program before but failed to follow through, that's okay. It just means you're more ready this time around. Don't look back at your mistakes; instead, look forward to your debt future. Today is a new day, and the time to start is now. Not to mention that this time you're armed with a new, foolproof guide: this book.

Start Above the Neck

Like all significant personal change, getting into debt begins with your mindset. Now that you've tackled your preconceptions about debt, it's time to get you thinking like a spender with two easy tweaks.

Imagine You're Rich

. . . and act like it. To start, make a few rich friends and observe their behaviors, such as how they handle a restaurant bill (throw down your credit card before anyone else can and let your dining companions know the meal is on you). As you begin to manifest your desires into reality, your rich friends will think you are generous and kind. They will want to go to dinner with you again and you will soon be locked into a delicious circle of reciprocity and companionship, with more opportunity to observe their lifestyle. You can also read books and watch movies about the wealthy, allowing their behaviors to settle into your fantasy life until you are able to act them out.

The more you practice being rich, the easier it will be to spend money like a rich person and, consequently, become a first-class debtor. Soon enough you'll use valet parking without a second thought, tipping on the way in *and* on the way out. You'll mention that Kobe beef tastes so much better than the best American rib-eye, and that Harry Winston is the go-to jeweler for diamonds. You'll be asking your friends for an introduction to their hard-to-get interior designer and lending them your nanny for a Saturday night out.

Harness Peer Pressure

While peer pressure usually has a negative connotation, when it comes to spending money, peer pressure is a useful motivator. There are two kinds of peer pressure: abstract and direct. Abstract peer pressure consists of "keeping up with the Joneses." You see others' lifestyles and belongings from afar and feel that you must maintain the pace. Your eyes *should* be open to others' possessions—how else will you know what, and how much, to buy?

Direct peer pressure occurs when your friends urge you to have fun and experience new things. You don't want to be a party pooper or a cheapskate, so when your next-door neighbors suggest a hot-air balloon and wine-tasting party, you pitch in and enjoy yourself. If what your friends are doing costs a little more money than you're used to, just charge it. It's only natural to want to participate *and* it will increase your debt.

The Power of Debt Thinking

You've just learned that pro-debt thinking is just as easy to embrace as the anti-debt propaganda you absorbed in your youth. Once you've accepted the appropriate mindset, there's no end to the debt you'll be able to accrue. Now it's time to look at the specifics and become an informed debtor. For example, have you ever stopped to question what debt actually is? In the next chapter, we'll take your hand and talk you through basic debt concepts that you may never have understood before.

CHAPTER 3
THE ABCs OF DEBT: DOING IT BY THE NUMBERS

NOW THAT YOUR HEART IS COMMIT-ted, it's time to get your brain up to speed. While most people think they know what debt is, in order to be a debt expert, it's helpful to review the basics, especially given the many misconceptions about deficit acquisition. In this chapter, we'll teach you some fundamental terms and concepts. To get on the road to debt, we need to intro-duce a few basic mathematical equations. Even if you were afraid of your high school algebra teacher and have a mental block when it comes to numbers, however, this book will walk you through the process step by step. You'll learn:

- How to "spend smart."

- A magical way to effortlessly increase debt.

- How to tell the difference between assets and debt.

- Whether your personal debt style is "country lane" or "autobahn."

What Is Debt?

The word *debt* dates to the fourteenth century, stemming from the Latin *debēr*, "to owe." In its early English uses, *debt* (then spelled *dette*), "something owed," did not necessarily imply money. Today, the "something owed" usually indicates a monetary commitment but can also encompass goods and services. While the word's earlier Biblical meaning meant "sin," fortunately the connotation has evolved since then.

In its contemporary definition, debt is the amount (in monetary terms or equivalent value of goods and services, because you may find yourself being requested to compensate in goods and services that which you borrowed in currency) that must be paid to an entity for borrowed funds. Debt can also refer to the state of owing, as in the phrase "I am in debt." The entity that extends the loan is said to be the *creditor*, while the borrower is the *debtor*. The lender *lends*, while the borrower *borrows*. The reciprocal complement of a *loan* is a *debt*. In its colloquial and practical incarnation, debt arises due to borrowing and overspending.

Progress Toward Debt

In order to borrow and spend enough to get into substantial debt, there are a few steps you'll want to take. While we'll explore exactly how to enact those steps in later chapters, for now we'll demonstrate the arithmetical concepts behind the process.

Step 1: Spend

Spend more than you earn. Once you've exhausted your income, accelerate your spending.

Wash Your Debt-Tablet in Water

Hammurabi, the best-known ruler of ancient Babylonia, reigned from around 1792 to 1750 BCE. He is recalled in large part for the code of law written under his watch. Though the Code of Hammurabi included primitive laws of retribution (including the first recorded instance of "an eye for an eye, a tooth for a tooth"), it was reasonable and forward-thinking on debt: "If any one owes a debt for a loan, and a storm prostrates the grain, or the harvest fail, or the grain does not grow for lack of water; in that year he need not give his creditor any grain, he washes his debt-tablet in water and pays no rent for this year."

Debt Equation 1: Overspending

Amount Spent – Income = Amount Overspent

Example: Madeleine earns $5,000 a month. Her monthly expenses amount to $6,000 per month. Therefore, Madeleine's overspending equals $1,000 per month.

Step 2: Borrow

How does Madeleine overspend her income? One possibility is to dip into savings, but that assumes that she has savings, and whatever savings she does have will run out eventually. The best way for Madeleine to overspend her income is to borrow money. To keep the math simple, we will assume that Madeleine does not have any savings.

Debt Equation 2: Borrowing

Amount to Borrow ≥ Amount Overspent

Example: The amount Madeleine will need to borrow must be greater than or equal to the amount by which she overspends, $1,000.

Step 3: Borrow More

If Madeleine is going to the trouble of taking out a loan (most likely in the form of credit cards) to fund her overspending, she may as well spend more, because once she's paying a monthly minimum on her credit cards, and once she's overspending to begin with, the "money" becomes imaginary.

Debt Equation 3: Borrowing More

Amount Borrowed + Income = Amount to Spend

Example: Madeleine earns $5,000 a month. Her monthly expenses amount to $6,000 per month. Since she's going to have to borrow money to fund the extra $1,000 per month, she may as well spend $2,000 extra per month.

Step 4: Build Cumulative Debt

Cumulative debt is not only the initial amount you borrowed, it's adjusted for repayments and includes interest, plus interest on the interest. As you spend the intangible money that debt

Words Disbursed

"I've never seen a Brink's truck follow a hearse to the cemetery."

—Barbara Hutton

bestows upon you, so does cumulative debt magically grow.

Debt Equation 4: Cumulative Debt

(Debt in period 1 – repayment in period 1) + (Interest on balance of debt – repayment in period 2 + newly acquired debt) + ... + (Interest on balance of debt from prior period(s) – repayment in current period + newly acquired debt) = Cumulative Debt

Example: Madeleine borrows $2,000 to overspend $2,000 each month. Every month she repays the minimum payment (3 percent of the current balance) of what she owes. The interest rate is 18 percent. The following table demonstrates what her cumulative debt will be in one year.

Month	Amount Borrowed	Prior Month's Balance	Current Balance	Interest*	Minimum Payment**	Cumulative Debt
1	$2,000	$0	$2,000	$0	$60	$1,940
2	$2,000	$1,940	$3,940	$30	$120	$3,850
3	$2,000	$3,850	$5,850	$60	$180	$5,730
4	$2,000	$5,730	$7,730	$90	$230	$7,590
5	$2,000	$7,590	$9,590	$110	$290	$9,410
6	$2,000	$9,410	$11,410	$140	$340	$11,210
7	$2,000	$11,210	$13,210	$170	$400	$12,980
8	$2,000	$12,980	$14,980	$200	$450	$14,730
9	$2,000	$14,730	$16,730	$220	$500	$16,450
10	$2,000	$16,450	$18,450	$250	$550	$18,150
11	$2,000	$18,150	$20,150	$270	$600	$19,820
12	$2,000	$19,820	$21,820	$300	$660	$21,460

Total borrowed: $24,000

Total accrued interest: $1,840

Total payments: $4,380

Total reduction in debt: $2,540

Total outstanding debt: $21,460

*Interest is calculated on prior month's balance. Rate is 18 percent annually, or 1.5 percent monthly.
**At 3 percent of current balance.

Madeleine borrowed a total of $24,000 over the course of one year. She made payments totaling $4,380 yet still owes $21,460 due to the accumulation of $1,840 in interest.

Your Net Worth

Now that you have learned the steps you need to take to increase your debt, you'll want to establish a financial baseline from which to target your future debt amount. This calculation is called "net worth," and equals the value of a person's assets, including cash, minus liabilities. In other words, it's what you own minus what you owe. While you want the number to be negative— meaning you want to owe more than you own—assets do come in handy as both collateral and proof of credit-worthiness when you are trying to get a loan to increase your debt.

To calculate your net worth, you'll need to make two lists: assets and liabilities. On the assets list, write everything you own in one column and its monetary value in another column. If you don't know an asset's value, just estimate it based on what you might be able to sell it for. On the debt list, note the same information, but for liabilities: loans, outstanding credit, and the amount of each. It should be relatively easy to figure out how much you owe, as lenders are quick to share that information with you.

Don't Feel Guilty

Businesses typically set aside 2 to 3 percent of net income as a reserve against bad debt, meaning it's solely there for the purpose of paying for you. Businesses are clearly accustomed to losing money in this way. Not only has the company already saved up to pay what you owe, its bad debt can be deducted when tax time rolls around.

Here are some examples of what you should include in these lists:

Financial Assets:

- Cash on hand
- Savings accounts
- Checking accounts
- Money-market accounts
- CDs
- Mutual funds
- Stocks
- Bonds
- Life insurance
- Pensions
- Prepaid expenses
- IRAs or other retirement plans

Tangible Assets:

- House (market value)
- Other real estate
- Automobiles
- Other personal items
- Clothing
- Jewelry
- Furniture

Debt:

- Outstanding bills
- Credit cards
- Mortgage
- Bank loans

- Student loans
- Car loans
- Other debt

Once you've made your lists, you can subtract debt from assets to determine your net worth.

Debt Equation 5: Net Worth

Assets – Liabilities = Net Worth

Example: Madeleine's assets total $1,000,000, and her debt is $800,000. Therefore her net worth is $200,000.

Remember that your goal is to have a *negative* net worth. The person with a net worth of $200,000 will have to spend money much more rapidly to catch up to the person who is starting this process with a net worth of -$200,000.

Your Debt-to-Income Ratio

Your net worth isn't the only measure of debt success. Debt-to-income ratio (DTI) compares how much you owe with how much you earn for a more dynamic calculation than net worth. There are different ways of measuring DTI, especially if you're applying for a mortgage. The equation below represents the broadest strokes of DTI.

Debt Equation 6: DTI

(Monthly Debt Payments) / (Monthly Income) = Debt-to-Income Ratio

Example: Madeleine's monthly household net income (after taxes and deductions) is $5,000. She pays $1,000 per month in credit card minimum payments, $2,000 per month for her mortgage (if Madeleine were a renter, her monthly rent would be included here instead), $500 in student loans, and $500 on a car loan, for a total of $4,000 in debt per month. Her debt-to-income ratio is therefore 80 percent.

Experts claim that a DTI over 50 percent is debt-aggressive, so Madeleine is on the right track!

The Speed of Debt

Now that you've established your net-worth starting point, it's time to take stock of your debt-acquisition style. There's more than one route to most destinations, and it's no different with debt: you can take the country lane or the autobahn. Most of us fall somewhere in between but tend toward one or the other.

Dollar Bills Are So Over

Who uses cash anymore? The poor dollar bill has only a 21-month life expectancy, which is why 45 percent of the $696 million in bills that the Bureau of Engraving and Printing produces *daily* are one-dollar notes. Of the 37 million currency notes printed every day, around 95 percent replace those that have been deemed unfit for circulation due to ripping and overall disintegration. Compare that to the piece of plastic in your pocket with its virtual non-biodegradability (you're more likely to lose it than harm it) and you'll understand why the United States is on the crest of the non-cash wave. In fact, of the total American paper currency in circulation (around $620 billion as of 2003), around 60 percent is held abroad by non-Americans who haven't caught up to the non-cash revolution.

Country Lane

If you're the type of person who likes to meander along the scenic route, you may want to select the winding country lane: the slow but inexorable accumulation of debt that grows over time. Just like you would watch your speed on a two-lane highway and enjoy the view, you nurture your debt carefully. You document how much you owe and take pride in watching your debt portfolio grow. You're choosy about your banker—she must understand you and cultivate your credit needs. You are impulsive in the sense that you will turn down an intriguing side road to explore, and your impulse purchases mimic that sensibility: you don't buy just anything, but instead make high-quality, thoughtful purchases.

Autobahn

If you prefer the fast lane on the autobahn, then you're a thrill seeker. You're in it for the ride, however long it lasts. You know there's the possibility that you'll crash and burn, but that's okay. When it comes to becoming a debtor, you're not concerned with paperwork. You want your loan and you want it now—from whoever will give it to you, at whatever rates. You're an exhilarated impulse buyer: you can't refuse yourself anything.

You Survived the Math

Congratulations—you're no longer a debt novice! After making your way through these challenging equations, you stand firmly at the intermediate level, knowledgeable about the terms that will allow you to increase your debt with finesse. Next we're going to take you one more time to the dark side—saving—but don't worry, because after that it's pure credit, debt, and spending!

CHAPTER 4
SAVING: DON'T DO IT

IMAGINE YOU'RE WALKING DOWN THE street, lost in a happy reverie picturing the piles of cash you've carefully saved over your lifetime. *SPLAT!* A bus hits you. Now what will you do with your hoarded fortune? Nothing. You're dead. You no longer have access to the joy that spending brings. Some people say, "Pass your wealth on to your children." What do *they* need it for? If you follow the guidelines in this book and teach them to your kids, they won't need your money; they'll do just fine getting into debt on their own. Besides, call it what you will—inheritance tax, estate tax, death duty—when you die, the IRS will take the lion's share of your assets. Translation: if you don't burn through your earnings—and then some—while you're alive, the government will have all your fun. Carpe spendem—buy today, die tomorrow!

But not to worry—if you adhere to the advice in this chapter, you'll kick the bucket with nary a penny in your pocket. Some of the concepts you're about to read will challenge long-held beliefs about saving, but that's what makes it interesting. We're about to show you:

- What can go wrong with banks.

- How socking money away will sabotage your debt plan.

- Who retirement plans benefit (hint: no one).

- Why 401(k)s and investments are risky.

Financial Institutions—Safe?

Most Americans believe that banks are impenetrably secure, and if they deposit their money, it will be there no matter what. But did you know that banks are only required to keep on hand as little as 3 percent of the money people have deposited? That means if everybody went to the bank to withdraw their money on the same day, 97 percent of us would be out of luck. And this is thanks to regulations set by the Federal Reserve.

This terrible scenario is exactly what happened after October 28, 1929, the Great Crash that led to the Great Depression. Following a period of historic prosperity, Wall Street sank to its knees in one horrible day. Because financial institutions invest deposits in the market, account holders scrambled

World's Greatest Miser

Known as the "Witch of Wall Street" for her penchant for wearing the same black dress (and the same underwear) every day, Hetty Green was the wealthiest American woman at the end of the nineteenth century—and the first woman to make her fortune through investing.

Though she turned an inheritance of around $7 million into more than $100 million by her death, she won the title of "World's Greatest Miser" from the *Guinness Book of World Records*. Green refused to turn on the heat or use hot water. She lived in a rundown apartment, reused envelopes, and was rumored to have spent an entire night searching for a 2-cent stamp. Her frugality was so severe that, on the basis of cost, she refused medical attention for her 14-year-old son when he dislocated his knee. After gangrene set in, his leg had to be amputated. Green again shunned treatment for her own hernia because the surgery cost $150.

But this story has a happy ending. Hetty's one-legged son went through his mother's money at the rate of $3 million a year after her death, funding his extravagant lifestyle, so at least it didn't *all* go to waste!

to withdraw their money all at once. But the crash ate as much as $140 billion in depositor money, and 9,000 banks failed. Even those who couldn't distinguish a stock from a rock were ruined.

Today, the Federal Reserve guarantees the safety of your wealth in the bank—but is anything foolproof? Better safe than sorry: if you spend your money immediately and intentionally you never have to worry about losing it due to someone else's mistakes. Not to mention that if there's another crash, your debts might be wiped out along with everybody else's assets!

Crash and Burn

The Great Crash erased over $5 billion worth of share values in just three days. By the end of 1929, $16 billion had been stripped from stock capitalization. It wasn't just millionaire traders who threw themselves off tall buildings, took up selling pencils on street corners, and moved into shantytowns. The Great Depression swallowed up nearly everyone—whether or not they'd ever purchased stocks.

If you want to crash and burn financially, there are more enjoyable ways to do so— one of this book's central premises. Would you rather go down in flames staring at plummeting numbers on a computer screen or soaking in a Jacuzzi tub in your custom-built dream home?

The Economic Pendulum

In addition to the vulnerability of the market itself, even minor fluctuations at the stock exchanges have the potential to erode the value of your dollar. Recession, inflation, and the ebb and flow of the economy can wreak havoc on your capital—if you save or invest it. While a dollar can devalue, can a vintage motorcycle? Or a diamond ring? Not only is monitoring the economy rather tedious, possessions will give you pleasure regardless of the Dow Jones.

Access Is Nine-Tenths of the Purchase

All saving strategies have one thing in common: they monopolize your money. Whether you call it a Keogh or a CD, a mutual fund or a bond, it's nothing more than a way for others to use your money instead of you. That's right—the reason why these instruments pay you that dangled incentive of paltry interest or earnings is because they are using your money for something else. It might be worthwhile if *they* were paying you the 22.95 percent interest you pay the credit card companies, but a savings account's paltry 1 or 2 percent? You're better off hiding it in a cigar box under the bed—at least there it's convenient to retrieve. Saving stalls the buying power of your cash—and in turn, your ability to achieve debt.

Savings Accounts

The most basic structure for tying up your money is the savings account. First, the saver relinquishes a sum of money to the bank. Modest (very low single-digit) interest accrues, but you can't even write a check against it. Opening a savings account will badly hamstring your quest for debt.

Debtor's Dictionary

spave: From *spend* + *save*. To spend money in order to save money on discounted items that you may or may not need. *Example*: Clyde sees a sweater for $25, marked down from $50. He was not planning on buying a sweater, but he can't pass up the bargain savings. Because it's such a fantastic deal, he buys two of them, and he's now saved $50—two times $25 in savings! Noun form: *spaver*, one who spaves.

Certificates of Deposit (CDs)

A more complex permutation of the savings account, a CD requires the saver to leave his money at the bank for a specified amount of time in exchange for a *slightly* higher interest rate—so that the institution knows how long it has to use his money. The longer the money is on deposit, the higher the interest rate. If the saver wishes to withdraw his cash before the CD "matures" (saver-speak for when he will once again be "allowed" access to his own money), he will be penalized. In the end, the saver *loses* money in his attempt to save it.

Mutual Funds

A mutual fund is a type of collective investment in which the fund manager invests pooled money into a diversified portfolio. The individual owns shares in the fund, which can be sold at any time. It sounds like a sure thing, but investing is an unpredictable endeavor, and mutual funds tend to perform *worse* than the stock market overall. Plus, who is this shady "fund manager" character? Do you know she'll charge a fee? Why pay someone else to mismanage your hard-earned cash?

Money-Market Deposit Accounts (MMDAs)

A money-market deposit account is one of the few savings entities that "allows" the account holder to write checks on her own money. This might sound like an upside, but MMDAs limit the number of monthly with-drawals—specifically, no more than six, and only three can be checks! As if that weren't enough of a deter-rent, MMDAs require a bigger initial deposit than other saving options. This means that you have to *save* to save—and you don't even want to save in the first place.

Retirement Plans

Proponents of saving argue that it's important to plan for the future. But would you rather have those designer stilettos now or when your feet are

---

Checks Are Bad

Nothing kills the spending mood faster than a check. You wait in line, annoy those behind you by taking the time to scribble out the info, hand over your driver's license and credit card (inappropriately used for identification purposes), and on top of all that the clerk will probably get a manager for approval. Checks are *over* in a big way, and if you use them for anything more than paying the minimum on your credit card bills, you're not a true debt embracer.

Unlike credit cards, checks are bound to the amount of money in your bank account. By using them, you lose the pleasure of consequence-free spending. If you bounce checks, you're charged a fee, and your name could be added to a database that will list you as a credit risk for other banks, lenders, and even potential employers. Avoid the check quagmire. Don't write—swipe!

---

too wrinkled and arthritic to squeeze into them? Life is about the present. Retirement plans have numerous drawbacks and will greatly hinder your bid for serious debt, so there's absolutely no need to go blind reading the fine print on conservative investments for your golden years. And chances are you'll have some kind of disease or early dementia before your benefits even have the chance to kick in. They say youth is wasted on the young. Don't waste yours!

401(k)s

The 401(k) is one of the most common retirement plans, a benefits option offered to employees of many medium- and large-sized companies. This instrument allows the worker to deposit up to 15 percent of his salary into the account—that's a 15 percent *decrease* in your spending allowance! If the employee withdraws his money before he reaches the age of 59 and a half (how arbitrary is *that*?), he will not only have to pay taxes on it, he'll be on the hook for a 10 percent IRS penalty. Here's another scenario that has you *losing* money in order to save it.

Another downside to the 401(k) is that the account holder himself is largely responsibly for managing the investments. The average employee is ill-equipped for this role and often fails to set aside enough funds each year. A recent Federal Reserve report notes that the average family's 401(k) account balance is only $29,000.

That's a shiny new car *now*, versus a diet of cat food when you retire!

IRAs and Keoghs

Individual Retirement Accounts (IRAs) and Keogh accounts are alternatives to the 401(k). While taxation and payment limits differ, these savings strategies are united by one principle: the capital is invested in stocks, bonds, mutual funds, and other opportunities. Whether you do it yourself or you pay somebody else to advise you, dabbling in the stock exchange always poses more risks than rewards. Plus, it's boring.

Home Equity: What's the Point?

Homes are good for one thing and one thing only: sheltering you in the manner to which you aspire. It's desirable to own your home because ownership gives you control over its renovation and decoration, but the equity you build is better extracted for spending—perhaps on a swimming pool, interior design, or something entirely undomestic, like a trip to Paris.

Savings in Disguise

The "equity" in your home is the difference between what your home is worth and how much you've paid off. That chunk of money just sits there, doing nothing for you. People mistakenly believe that increasing their home equity (by making a larger down

Debtor's Dictionary

granny bank: Old-fashioned savings accounts created by grandparents to fund their grandchildren's education, first home purchase, and other expenses, distributed via *grandspending*.

payment or by making higher principal payments) means they are wisely investing in their future. Home equity is nothing more than another savings plan. Don't leave that equity stagnating in your home; instead, harness the power of your equity to finance your lifestyle. Here's how: when you do accumulate some equity—for example, because your home's value has increased—take out a Home Equity Line of Credit (HELOC) and spend what's rightfully yours.

Reverse Mortgages

If you're over 62 years old and you've made the mistake of building equity in your home, there's a way to make it right: take out a reverse mortgage. A senior homeowner borrows an amount up to the value of her home, paid out by the lender to the homeowner in monthly tax-free payments. When the homeowner sells the house or dies, the house is usually sold, and the bank is compensated for the sum it paid out—and then some. By the time you die, you will hopefully have enjoyed spending all of the equity in your house.

Words Disbursed

"Money is just the poor man's credit card."
                                    —Marshall McLuhan

A Penny Saved Is...
Just a Penny

To be a debt embracer it's also necessary to be an independent thinker. While most of the world is moving in the debt direction, many habits and concepts still die hard. The "virtue" of saving is one of those stubborn dinosaurs—no matter how much evidence to the contrary, people still believe in it. Fortunately, you now understand why saving will do nothing but impede your spending frenzy *and* potentially cost you money. But how exactly are you going to finance your ideal lifestyle? Next we tackle credit cards—the late-twentieth-century innovation that will finance your dreams and build your debt.

NOW OFFERING
UNLIMITED CREDIT
34.999%*
INTEREST
JUST FOR YOU!
*
CREDIT
VISA

CHAPTER 5
CREDIT CARDS: THE PLASTIC HIGH-LIFE

WE MAY HAVE MYSTIFIED SOME OF you with all this talk about spending, spending, spending. How, you've been asking, will I *pay* for it? Your understanding of debt and the detrimental impact of spending have served as mere preambles for what we are about to share with you: credit cards are the key to life.

You'll recall from chapter 3 that:

Spending – Income = Overspending ≤ Borrowing

Many debt novices don't think credit cards constitute borrowing. It's true that with credit, if you don't use it, you don't borrow anything; it represents only the *possibility* of borrowing. Once you charge a set of golf clubs on that zero-balance potential for a loan, however, you've borrowed money. And that's when you're off to the races.

When you incorporate borrowing as a means of supporting your dream life, you free yourself from having to earn as much money as you spend. You'll want to avail yourself of different types loans. Here we'll discuss credit cards, and in chapter 6, we'll tackle other kinds of loans. Credit cards are by far the best instruments for daily lifestyle improvement, and in this chapter you'll learn:

- How credit cards originated with the desire to dine.

- How many credit card offers you can expect in your mailbox, and which ones you should respond to (hint: all of them).

- Why you don't need to read your card-holder agreements.

- Why debit cards are evil.

Credit Cards 101

The first credit cards were house accounts issued by individual companies—gas stations, hotel chains, department stores—and date largely to the 1920s. The first charge card—"charge" rather than "credit" because the balance had to be paid off in full every month, the Diners Club card, was introduced in 1950 by businessmen seeking more convenient ways to entertain clients in restaurants. The Diners Club concept differed from the house account cards because it introduced an intermediary that paid the establishment, which then billed the customer.

Credit Card Microtransactions

Vending machines are such a hassle. Either you don't have the right change or your barely wrinkled dollar bill gets spit out no matter how delicately you reinsert it. Those days will soon be over—companies have become increasingly aware of the benefit of these "microtransactions," and vending machines that take credit cards are coming. A USA Technologies survey shows that buyers spend 50 percent more at vending machines offering cashless payment. According to the report, "Studies prove that consumers are less price sensitive when making purchases with their credit card, and sales losses due to out-of-change conditions are minimized when credit systems are introduced." Grab a snack and get into debt!

American Express augmented its traveler's checks with credit cards in 1958, the same year that Bank of America launched the BankAmericard in California; BankAmericard was licensed for use in other states in 1966 and renamed Visa in 1976. MasterCard emerged out of multiple mergers and new names, including "Master Charge" from 1969 until 1979. Revolving credit was one the cards' innovations, whereby a cardholder is approved up to a certain limit but can carry a balance, which partially determines the extent of fees and interest charges.

In 1943, the total outstanding consumer credit in the United States was $6.6 billion—by 2007, that figure had ballooned to $2.4 trillion. As of 2004, no fewer than 1.3 billion credit cards were circulating through the wallets and stores of the United States, 44 percent of which were Visa and Master-Card accounts. That's over 4 credit cards per American citizen—including children.

The mechanics of credit cards are simple. A consumer fills out an application. A financial institution extends a line of credit to the consumer based upon the financial information in the application. The financial institution sends a small piece of plastic adorned with a magnetic strip, an account number, and the cardholder's name. Then cardholders swipe their plastic rectangles in card-reader machines to make purchases or obtain cash advances. The financial institution pays the retail entity and bills the cardholder.

As of March 2007, total revolving debt in the United States was $888.2 billion, or more than $7,990 per household, and it's no wonder: credit cards provide instant gratification. You can make your purchases now even if you don't have the money. They're convenient because you don't have to carry cash, they're faster than writing a check, and they're accepted almost anywhere. They are small and thus eminently portable.

Credit cards are a miracle of the modern age. You will want to take advantage of all the benefits offered by credit cards by having many of them. You'll use them for everyday purchases as well as big splurges. You'll employ balance transfers to pay off one card with another, shuffling your debt around to your advantage (see chapter 9, "Avoiding Payback: Bills, Collections, and Bankruptcy").

Check Your Mailbox

Credit cards have never been more available. In 2005, over 6 billion credit card offers

Credit Cards and Your Children

It's important to teach your children to use credit at the earliest possible ages. You can give them a credit card with their name on it by making them an "authorized user" on your account, which means they can use the card but have no obligation to pay its bills. Most credit card companies have no minimum age requirement for authorized users.

As far as getting their own accounts, kids have to wait until they're legally liable adults at the age of 18—though some credit card companies are experimenting with going younger. Fortunately, credit cards are distributed freely and aggressively to college students. Today's coeds are getting a head start on debt!

	Freshman	Sophomore	Junior	Senior
Percentage who have credit cards	54%	92%	87%	96%
Average number of cards	2.5	3.67	4.5	6.13
4 or more cards	26%	44%	50%	66%
Average credit card debt	$1,533	$1,825	$2,705	$3,262

From "Undergraduate Students and Credit Cards: An Analysis of Usage Rates and Trends," Nellie Mae, April 2002.

were sent in the mail to around 75 percent of all American households (the other 25 percent, presumably, languish under the dark cloud of non-credit-worthiness)—that's over 55 offers per household that received them! Sooner or later you will receive solicitations in the mail, all of which you should answer promptly.

At the same time, you should be aggressive and seek out the best cards for you. It's best to do that online, using sites like BankRate.com, Creditcards.com, Card-Offers.com, or Cardweb.com. On one given day, for example, Creditcards.com was offering 25 instant-approval cards.

Concerned about your credit? The credit card companies aren't. In 2007, Bank of America announced that they would issue credit cards to people without social security numbers, targeting illegal immigrants who have been unable to establish credit. "If we don't disproportionately grow in the Hispanic [market]," a Bank of America official told the *Wall Street Journal*, "we aren't going to grow." Applications are approved as long the aspiring debtors have held a positive amount in a Bank of America bank account for three months—and they even get to pay over 21 percent in interest. Pretty soon you won't even need a real address to get a credit card!

Credit Card Terms Defined

Whatever types of credit cards you decide to obtain, they all have similar features: daily balances, grace periods, minimum payments, and so on. As a debt embracer, you'll want to understand what they are and how they can or can't help you get into debt.

Feature	What It Is	Value to a Debt Embracer
Annual Fee	Some cards charge fees once per year for the privilege of using the card.	Not much. The annual fee is tiny compared to the amount you'll be spending.
Annual Percentage Rate (APR)	Percentage rate charged by companies on outstanding balances. Can be variable (changing according to such factors as federal interest rates) or fixed.	Very high. You'll want to get the lowest possible interest rates in order to keep your debt going for as long as possible.
Balance-Transfer Options	Ability to move the balance of one card to another.	Very high. You can increase your debt while extending its life. Debt should be managed like a shell game, balancing transfers frequently (see chapter 9).
Charge-Off	When a creditor doesn't think a balance will be paid, it "charges off" the amount, closes the account, and still tries to collect the debt.	High. The last thing you want is your credit card to be closed. Avoid this by submitting the minimum payment on time.
Daily Balance	Usually expressed as an average: the total balance is divided by the number of days in the month-long billing cycle. Interest is based on this amount.	Low. It's more important just to spend what you want to spend, and debt embracers won't be paying balances anyway.
Grace Period	Time during which no interest is charged on an unpaid balance from the day an item is charged (not from the day the bill is due).	Negligible. A debt embracer will never pay a balance off during the grace period.

Minimum Payment	Minimum monthly amount a cardholder must pay on an account, usually 2 to 3 percent of the total outstanding balance.	Very high. You must *always* pay the minimum payment, on time, or your ability to attain more credit will be impaired.
Misc. Fees	Lenders charge fees for various discrepancies, including late payments and going over the credit limit. Cash advances usually carry a fee, as does charging in a foreign currency.	Moderate. While these can add up, they are usually not a huge percentage of your balance. However, late payments can wreak other problems.

Choosing a Card

You should choose a card according to its costs and benefits. In terms of interest rates, selecting low rates will allow you to take on more credit and sustain it for longer periods of time. As your debt grows, however, you may find that only higher interest rates are available to you: take them.

Do choose cards according to the benefits they offer. If your dream lifestyle includes travel, get credit cards that reward your

Represent Yourself

Personalizing your credit card is a terrific way to express yourself and add flavor to your purchasing routine. When you apply for "affinity cards" from organizations that reflect your interests, your plastic, emblazoned with a logo, becomes a microcosm of your whole identity. Boast about your alma mater every time you swipe, or show that retailer which team will go all the way!

If style is your main concern, a company called CreditCovers can up the ante. They make "skins," credit card slipcovers with hip designs. Go minimalist by choosing the solid white or black, choose the wallpaper look of the "Ohmigawd!" style, or make an ironic retro nod to cash with a skin that reproduces a $100 bill.

spending with frequent-flyer miles. If you want some help making your minimum payments, apply for a rebate card. If you want to pay homage to your university, get an "affinity" card, which is issued by a bank in conjunction with an organization and branded with the organization's logo.

> ## Black Power
>
> The American Express Centurion is the card
> you can't apply for. The legendary black card—
> forged in titanium, not plastic—is available by
> invitation only to customers who charge more
> than $250,000 per year. Delivered in a velvet-
> lined box, the card requires a $5,000 initiation
> fee and a $2,500 annual fee. In return, card-
> holders get personal concierge service, airline
> upgrades and other travel perks, and the right
> to plop down a status symbol to buy (according
> to one company-reported purchase) a Bentley.
> Remember—the more you charge, the more
> likely it is you'll get a black card!

If the organization is a nonprofit, it will
sometimes receive a percentage of sales on
the card, but this is largely irrelevant. Premium cards—such as gold or platinum—are
most desirable, as they offer higher credit
limits and shopping incentives.

Whatever you do, avoid debit cards. No
matter how they disguise themselves, these

are *not* credit cards, as they link directly to your checking account and are thus limited to the amount of money you actually have. The aspiring debtor wants to avoid using cash whenever possible.

Plastic Is the New Paper

The most significant rule of thumb when it comes to credit cards is "The more, the merrier." Anything beyond that is mumbo-jumbo. Because the *informed* debtor can achieve ever higher volumes of debt, this journey through the specifics of credit card usage will prove invaluable as you open the many credit-offering envelopes that cross your transom. While credit cards are the kings of debt accumulation, only the knee-jerk debtor would deny all resources at his disposal. In the next chapter, we'll explore other types of loans.

CHAPTER 6
OTHER TYPES OF LOANS: DON'T DENY THE NON-PLASTIC

FOR MOST PEOPLE, CREDIT CARDS constitute the first step in establishing personal credit. Once you've established a successful track record with the plastic, you're ready to build your loan portfolio. Consumers suffer under the misconception that banks do them a favor by lending money. The truth is that loans are major profit centers for banks, so bankers are eagerly waiting for you to walk in their door. Take advantage of your position as a buying customer and demand the money you want (politely, of course.) And if you can't find a banker who's willing to make a deal, there are plenty of others who are. Hold on to your Aeron chair and fasten your Gucci belt, because you're about to learn:

- What to consider when choosing a college or university.

- What to do if you can't afford to buy the car of your dreams.

- How to simplify your first home purchase.

- Little-known ways of obtaining loans from unusual sources.

Never Worry About Payback

Because you will either get another loan or find another solution, as a debt embracer you should never concern yourself with how you will repay your loans. While accepting the fact that someday the loans may be called in, you have the confidence that you will always map a way out (see chapter 9, "Avoiding Pay-back: Bills, Collections, and Bankruptcy"). The twin goals of acquiring more debt and spending more money are enough to think about without having to contemplate something theoretical and far away. The worst thing a debt embracer can do is allow worries to detract from her chosen lifestyle.

Identity Thieves Will Steal Your Debt

According to the Federal Trade Commission, as many as 9 million Americans are victims of identity theft each year—one person every 4 seconds, to the tune of $50 billion in losses. With identity theft, someone fraudulently opens credit cards and other accounts in your name, then makes purchases for which they never intend to pay, leaving you holding the bag. What's worse, identity thieves can ruin your credit rating, thereby diminishing your ability to apply for new credit cards and loans. Don't be a victim: monitor your accounts and check your credit report regularly or else careless strangers will have all your fun. It's *your* debt, not theirs!

Always Go Long-Term

For the debt embracer, terms on bank loans (meaning the length of time between taking out the loan and perhaps having to pay it back) should always be as long as possible. This will decrease your monthly payments because you have more months to divide into the total amount. While it's always better to have the lowest-possible interest rate, it's more important to go with the loans that will get you access to the most money over the longest period of time.

Types of Loans

In their broadest strokes, loans are targeted to different life stages. Many people start with a student loan, graduate to an auto loan, then continue on to a mortgage. Once you have the mortgage and thus some collateral, you can take out such personal loans as HELOCs (see chapter 4, "Saving: Don't Do It").

Academy of Debt

College is one of the gateways to adulthood. When considering a life of debt, it's important to note that student loans are a great place to start: no prior credit history is required, they help establish good credit, they're given to anyone who is enrolled in college, and over $134 billion is available.

Not to mention that college is good for you, or, if that ship has already sailed, for your children. Because college is so much more than books and studies, you'll want to choose a private institution or at the very

> ### Debtor's Dictionary
>
> **liar loan:** Loan or mortgage granted on the basis of "stated income" (without supporting documentation to verify borrower's claims).

least one that's out of state. Living at home will retard your maturation, and you'll definitely need a car. Once you're in school, live like the person you want to be: an actor, personal assistant, or rock star.

As for graduate school, yes, yes, and yes. Follow your creative dream and take out loans whether or not there are any paid career opportunities at the other end. You have the right to express yourself, regardless of whether the market values your work with something as crass as the almighty dollar. But neither do you have to make any sacrifices in your lifestyle. After all, starving artists are *so* last century.

Your First Car

After college, the day will come when the car your parents bought you breaks down or, worse, becomes unfashionable. This means it's time to get a new car—not a "new to you" car, but a new car. Which car you choose is one of the most important decisions you'll make in your early life, as your car reflects your social status, so you need something sexy and luxurious. If you're having trouble getting a loan for the car you want, you may want to consider leasing. Because you don't own the vehicle, however, you won't build credit for your next big purchase or expand your debt portfolio. Leasing is a positive for those who want lower monthly payments and a new car every two or three years—rather than going through the trouble of selling it, you can just drop it off at the dealership!

Not Worth Its Metal

In the annals of "Cash is so passé," it now costs 1.4 cents to make a penny. That's right: pennies are worth more as metal than as currency. In 1982, copper prices rose and production was shifted to copper-coated zinc; since 2003, however, the price of zinc has skyrocketed. Because almost 60 percent of Americans take pennies out of circulation, sequestering them in coin jars and even throwing them away, penny production has *risen* over recent years. Despite being officially called a "nuisance coin," multiple bills in Congress to abolish the denomination have failed and polls show that nearly two-thirds of Americans want the penny to stay. Debt embracers, clearly, comprise the other noble third.

Home Sweet Home

After you've gone to school and bought a car, choosing your dream home is the next step. Although renting can be consistent with the free-wheeling, fancy-free attitude of the debtor, buying a house is an unparalleled way to build debt. By mid-2006, outstanding mortgage debt was at an all-time high of $9 trillion. Mortgage expenses continue to take up a larger chunk of American's disposable income, at over 11.5 percent. And, with the exception of yachts and catastrophic medical events, it's impossible to rack of hundreds of thousands (if not millions) of dollars of debt with just one purchase.

Before you start house-hunting, list everything you could possibly want in a house. Write down your desired number of bedrooms and bathrooms, the brand of appliances and the type of marble you want in the kitchen, the shape of the pool, etc. Don't worry about what you can afford: that's what the mortgage is for.

When it's time to secure that mortgage, prioritize a low (or, better yet, zero) down payment and a long payoff period over a low interest rate. Even if your credit is less than stellar, don't worry, there are still plenty of entities that cater to customers like you—their ads tend to begin, "Bad Credit? No Problem!"

If you don't have money for a down payment, there are government programs and loans for 103 percent of the

The Loan Shark

The lenders of last resort, loan sharks should be consulted only after all your borrowing options have been exhausted—including payday loans, the contemporary equivalent old-time loan sharks. Today loan-sharking is far more visible in Asia than in the United States, but if you're in trouble, there's always a way to make it worse. You'll need to do some asking around: loan sharks operate within poor immigrant communities, help fund shady or illegal businesses such as strip clubs, and participate in organized crime.

The nineteenth century and early twentieth century marked the heyday of popular loan-sharking. Because legitimate loans were only available to the wealthy, loan sharks and pawnbrokers played significant roles in working-class communities. The activities of loan sharks were defined as illegal primarily by usury laws setting maximum interest rates at 6 percent; instead, loan sharks charged 20 to 300 percent, with smaller loans drawing higher rates. Around 1900, as many as one in five American workers owed a loan-shark debt.

Today physical harm can indeed come from unpaid loan-shark debt, but they're unlikely to kill you—then you'd never pay them back.

property value (to cover closing costs). Stated-income loans, no-income-verification loans, and no-document loans all exempt you from having to prove either employment or credit history.

Once you're in your home, guess what? The process isn't over. Not only is your house is an endless opportunity to spend money, you'll no doubt be looking to upgrade in no time.

Other Ways to Get Money

A traditional savings and loan isn't the only player in the money game. Besides getting creative with a mortgage, here are some other great options:

- **Insurance-policy loan:** You can borrow against the value of your life-insurance policy, up to the value of that policy.

- **Payday loan:** If you're short on cash
  and payday is days away, seek this
  short-term, high-interest (with APRs
  as high as 912 percent!) loan. The pri-
  mary drawback to payday loans is they
  rarely go over $1,500, but you can take
  out as many as you need and they're
  available online.

- **Friends and family:** If you're lucky
  enough to have friends and family with
  cash to spare, by all means, hit them up!
  They're usually reluctant to ask you about
  payback, so never bring it up yourself.

The Money's Rolling In

Congratulations, debtor—you're set up! Now there's only one thing to do: spend, spend, then spend some more. In the next two chapters, we're going to show you all the ways you can spend more money than you ever thought possible, from mindless daily expenses to huge impulse buys. This is truly the fun part, so enjoy!

EXPENSES FALL INTO ONE OF TWO categories: overhead and discretionary purchases. Overhead expenses largely stay constant, irrespective of your day-to-day activities or spending habits, while discretionary expenses change with impulses and amount of use. Overhead includes such recurring bills as rent or mortgage, car payments, and insurance; these expenses are collectively known as your "monthly nut."

Trying to get into debt requires different approaches for the two types of expenses. For overhead, you'll want to focus on cultivating luxury and implementing a life of ease. Big-ticket items like a condo on the beach or convertible sports car guarantee a high monthly mortgage and car payments. Hiring staff to service your life—house-keeper, gardener, personal trainer, life coach—awards you with large ongoing bills. Memberships, tuition, and time-shares will also accomplish your goals. Even if your monthly bills right now are woefully low and you're flying under the radar of con-sumer culture, this chapter will bring you up to speed, showing you:

- How to turn your "wants" into "needs."

- The unexpected benefits of renting.

- Why you should never turn out a light.

- How easy it can be to clean up after a pet.

Turn Wants into Needs

One person's "luxury" is another's necessity, and your job as a debt embracer is to view everything you desire as an absolute requirement. No one has the right to decide for someone else what is necessary or what is wasteful; you deserve only the best.

Needs and wants can, however, be difficult to distinguish. Debt deniers believe it's mandatory to live as small a life as possible, merely subsisting on the cheapest "basic" needs. As a debt embracer, you are confident enough to indulge your instincts, whether they belong to that unreasonably narrow category of items "necessary to biological function," such as gruel, water, air, and elements-deflecting shelter, or they reflect the evolved human need to express oneself through lifestyle.

It couldn't be easier to transform your wants into needs: if you want it, you need it! Life is simpler when you have only one category of urge. The right to satisfy all impulses takes away so much of life's onerous decision-making—"Should I do it?" "Should I get it?" "Do I deserve it?" Yes!

Your Home

Whether you rent or own, your home is not only castle, sanctuary, and self-expression, it's a great place to spend money on a monthly basis. Some people choose to live in unacceptably inelegant surroundings in order to maintain their "discretionary" lifestyle—going out to eat, owning beautiful clothing, etc. Others sacrifice their home for their car. And still others are "house rich, cash poor," sacrificing their ability to enjoy themselves in order to reside in a gorgeous

Your Own McMansion

What better reason to get into debt than to erect your own McMansion? Despite the shrinking of the average household size in the United States, from 4.76 people in 1900 to 2.72 in 2000, the average house keeps growing. After World War II, homes were about 900 square feet; by 1970, this had increased to 1,400 square feet, and in 2006, 2,300 square feet. But *you* won't be satisfied with anything less than 5,000 square feet, the typical McMansion size in 2007—up from 3,000 just 10 years ago!

McMansions are generally built in planned communities, often by the pioneering Toll Brothers builders. Homes are "customized" rather than "custom," meaning the buyer picks and chooses from among various options. Potential styles include Tudorbethan, French château, and Mediterranean. Trends point to a "great room" (combined living and dining areas opening to a huge kitchen), whirlpool tubs in enormous bathrooms, ample laundry rooms, and at least four bedrooms. Once you move in, you'll be able to call your home by a variety of nicknames: plywood palazzo, faux chateau, garage Mahal, starter castle, pocket mansion, or luxury move-up home (the Toll Brothers' preferred designation).

dwelling. The debtor, however, refuses to make these choices.

As outlined in chapter 6, the homeowner debt embracer will choose the mortgage that requires the smallest possible output of cash, then will extract equity from the house as it builds. For renting debtors, various tempting choices exist. Because no down payment is required for rentals, renting frees chunks of cash that could better be spent elsewhere. You can always take cash advances on your credit cards to pay your rent. Additionally, in a sign of progress, landlords are increasingly accepting credit cards for payment!

Overall, even if your income isn't what you wish it was, don't sacrifice your home comfort. Go for the biggest home you can afford by borrowing to the max.

Your Utilities

While utilities will comprise a small percentage of your overall spending, it is nonetheless important to overcome a few anti-debt tendencies, as follows:

- **Electricity:** It's inconvenient to think about turning lights and appliances off; don't bother.

- **Water:** Long showers, giant bathtubs, and a swimming pool are your right. Green lawns look best no matter your climate, so install them and water them to perfection.

- **Cable:** It is inhumane to expect anyone to live without HBO.

- **Telephone:** Though telephone deregulation has allowed for more consumer choice, it's a hassle the debtor doesn't need. Whether choosing a local, long-distance, or cellular plan, use whatever plan the company recommends, regardless of your usage habits. If your habits change, don't hassle yourself with calling to modify your plan.

- **Heat and air-conditioning:** Leave them on, even if you're not home. Who wants to come home to a cold house in the winter and a warm one in the summer?

Your Family

If you deserve the best, doesn't your family? Since you've already committed to a top-notch home in a great neighborhood, you've made a good start. Of course, no child should have to go to public school—and fortunately, many private schools now accept credit cards. Hobbies should be encouraged,

> ## Debtor's Dictionary
>
> *inconspicuous affluence*: Expression of wealth in which riches are, oddly, played down, sometimes to suggest lower-than-actual socioeconomic status, generally due to misplaced shame.
>
> *conspicuous austerity*: Spending large amounts of money on items and services that appear inexpensive and simple (with prices rising in proportion to perceived simplicity of purchases, as with ashrams and black cashmere sweaters), often to satisfy twisted definitions of virtue; or intentionally attempting to convey a lower-than-actual socioeconomic status.
>
> *stealth wealth*: Manifestation of riches characterized by deliberately understated but extremely expensive activities and belongings which eschew visible labels and are identifiable as extravagant only to those in the know.

horses acquired and tended, and designer labels indulged. Skiing is a birthright. (More on these discretionary expenses in chapter 8.) Your children will have their own cell phones and, in time, their *own* credit cards. Remember that your offspring reflect on you, and you want to instill in them debt-embracing attitudes that they, in turn, will pass on to their children.

Your Support Staff

There are two types of people in this world: debt embracers and those who live within their means. As a debt embracer, you want to hire some of those who live within their means to work for you. This will not only increase your monthly nut and improve your lifestyle, it will help contribute to those less fortunate—though this is a secondary consideration. Most true debt embracers find they cannot live without the following:

- **Personal trainer:** To best wear designer clothing, you need to be fit, and, because of your driving- and valet-oriented lifestyle, this is difficult, if not impossible, to accomplish on your own. Whether your personal trainer visits you at home or conducts sessions at the gym, you'll need a professional to guide you through your repetitions—at least bi-weekly, if not daily.

- **Therapist:** Sometimes you will lose out on the opportunity to buy the latest Jimmy Choos or limited-edition BMW. Or, you may experience denial of credit, a challenge that can be overcome with emotional support. A good therapist is thus a necessity.

- **Nanny:** If you have children, you will certainly require the services of a nanny to free you up for shopping and recreation. Try a live-in arrangement, as this will require less cash outflow but yield more childcare time.

- **Housekeeper:** With all your time spent cultivating your debt, you cannot be expected to clean your own house. A professional will also yield better results.

- **Gardener:** The days when dads spent the weekend mowing the lawn and trimming the hedges are long gone. These jobs are now gladly assumed by those lower on the American Dream ladder.

- **Dog-waste remover:** A thrilling new industry has been created by those who prefer to let others handle their shit. These services will come to your house two or three times a week, leaving your yard excrement-free while still allowing you to enjoy canine companionship.

Your Life

It's hard work both bringing in an income *and* overspending it. Thankfully, there's plenty of recreation to be experienced that has the added bonus of increasing your overhead:

- **Pets:** Pets are a great way to spend money, and they give you nonverbal love in exchange. With expenses from food to grooming to vet bills, you'll want at least two or three furry companions.

Diagnosis: Oniomania

If you have a compulsive urge to make sense-less purchases and you experience distress if your spending itch isn't scratched, then you might be the lucky victim of oniomania. From the Greek *ōnios*, "to be bought," and *ōnos*, "price," oniomania affects approximately 1.8 percent of Americans and has been known to interfere with daily life. Debt-embracing oniomaniacs, however, can take comfort in the knowledge that they will never stray from their debt plans—it's hard-wired.

- **Groceries:** While you'll mostly be dining out or using takeout (see chapter 8, "Discretionary Spending: Impulse Buys and Designer Labels"), when you do shop for groceries, patronize gourmet stores like Whole Foods or use last-minute convenience stores. Buy food that represents good intentions (fruit, vegetables, fish) then let it rot in the fridge because you instead opt for pizza.

- **Gas:** Live far from your workplace and choose your car based on pleasure and status (see below), then spend what you must on fuel.

- **Gym membership:** Whether or not you consider the gym to be leisure, go for amenities that help take away the pain of exercising, such as valet parking, laundry service, private lockers, and massage services.

- **Club membership:** Most debt embracers will benefit from some kind of club membership, such as golf, country, or tennis. Not only will your memberships provide recreation, they will also put you into contact with others of similar values.

Your Transportation

The debt embracer knows that an automobile does much more than carry her from point A to point B. Where homes privately reflect lifestyle and affluence, cars publicly proclaim one's commitment to the appearance of success.

Fortunately, whether you purchase or lease, cars are one area for which credit is easy to attain. *Never* buy a car outright when financing is so readily available. When you choose a car, remember how much it reflects on you when you are out and about in the world. Pay no attention to fuel efficiency, as that may prevent your driving the car of your dreams, not to mention that it's easy to charge gasoline.

A Cracked Nut

We've just demonstrated how easy it is to increase your monthly overhead with outflow for both the mundane and the exotic. While there are natural limits to your overhead options, discretionary spending opens boundless possibilities for accumulating debt. In chapter 8, we'll explore the moment-to-moment choices you'll make to improve your debt levels *and* happiness.

CHAPTER 8
DISCRETIONARY SPENDING: IMPULSE BUYS AND DESIGNER LABELS

WHEN IT COMES TO SPENDING, DIScretionary purchases are where the real fun and creativity start. Putting a roof over one's head and making a car payment can become routine (even if it *is* a mock Tudor or a Mercedes), but discretionary spending is always about instant gratification. For the debtor, as outlined in chapter 7, *want* equals *need*. If you've got a desire, it must be satisfied. Anti-debt propaganda preaches the gospel of delayed gratification, there's little actual point to such self-denial. The future and the past do not exist: if you want something now, you should have it. The purchase of luxury goods has grown four times faster than total purchases in recent years because people like to shine and be noticed. Whether ordering a second bottle of wine, spraying on a fake tan, or jetting off to a much-deserved vacation, we'll show you how to go into debt discretion by discretion. You'll learn:

- How to accept the "upsell."

- How to comparison-shop for more expensive choices.

- How to make around-the-clock purchases.

- How to allow Starbucks to grow your debt.

Shopping like a Pro

For the debt embracer, shopping is a carefully acquired skill. Not everybody can turn small daily purchases into debt. While shopping is undoubtedly enjoyable, the debtor

> ## Retail Therapy
>
> Researchers believe that the act of shopping can release serotonin into the brain, a natural chemical that alleviates depression and causes spenders to experience feelings of tranquility, euphoria, and ecstasy. So make the most of it—whenever you feel down, go buy something.

must approach discretionary spending as a serious endeavor, for only then will debt grow at the desired velocity. While we will soon outline the different categories of discretionary spending, first you should become familiar with several principles that apply overall.

Tempus Fugit

When you see something you want, don't wait. Time is fleeting, and if you wait until tomorrow it may be gone. Whether the item is a La Perla bustier, a LeRoy Nieman that matches your living room sofa, or a diamond-studded Rolex, there's no time like the present. Get it—don't regret it.

The Beauty of the Splurge

Big splurges are *always* a good bet, to be indulged no matter the price tag. Perhaps you've been wanting a new digital camera and you happen to walk past an electronics shop. The clerk shows you a multiple-megapixel camera with a set of lenses for $9,999. Do not blink. Do not pass go. Just buy it.

Think Appearances

Staying hip and happening will help you along your path to debt. Subscribe to such publications as *Forbes*, *Vogue*, *Architectural Digest*, and *GQ* and shop accordingly. These magazines will guide you to what's new, hot, chic, important—and expensive.

Buy Top-Tier

When you have a choice between low, medium, and high quality, always go high. Contrary to your pre-debt-embracing practice, you'll want to compare price tags in order to determine whether something is good enough for you. If it's too cheap, this is a strong sign that it's not worthy and you should go with the more expensive item.

Make Rich Friends

Rich people spend a lot of money without thinking about it, and spending time with them will help you do the same.

> ## Debtor's Dictionary
>
> **snob effect**: Dynamic whereby higher prices lead to higher demand (contrary to standard economics of low prices leading to high demand) due to perceived social status.

Always Take the Upsell

We've all experienced the upsell, a salesperson's effort to help us spend more money. Whether it's an extended warranty sponsored by the store, protective upholstery spray at the car wash, or the classic "Would you like fries with that?" query, always accept. If you're dealing with an inexperienced clerk who forgets to dangle the upsell, gently prompt him with a comment like "Do you think there's anything else I need?"

Half-off? Hands off!

The debt embracer doesn't even consider buying on sale. Not only are sale events attended by hordes of déclassé competitive shoppers, sale items go on sale for a reason: lackluster demand, defects, or expired seasonality.

Never Use Cash

We've mentioned it elsewhere, but it bears repetition: cash is *not* a tool of the debtor. It's inconvenient (not only does it makes you a target of crime, it's incredibly easy to lose, and once it's gone, there's no one to call for a replacement), but the real deterrent to cash is its finite nature. Cash creates an artificial sense of spending limits. You might reach into your wallet, see you don't have enough for

that antique grandfather clock, and
decide not to buy it. Wrong! That's
why there are credit cards.

Discretionary Categories

When it comes to discretionary spending,
you'll mostly concentrate your efforts in one
of four areas: dining and entertainment,
fashion and hygiene, home décor, and vacations. Personal tastes will dictate whether
one arena becomes more important than
the others, but successful debt acquisition
almost always requires some activity in all
four of the sectors. If one of them isn't your
style, not to worry, because we'll help you
find a way to overextend yourself.

Dining and Entertainment

Some people reserve eating out for
special occasions, or distinguish

between daily eateries and splurge restaurants. The debt embracer doesn't bother with such categorization. If you don't feel like cooking, head out for sushi. If you crave prime rib, what's stopping you? While at times you may choose to forgo alcohol for health reasons, in general you should always accompany your meal with a fine bottle of wine—preferably selected by the restaurant's sommelier. Let him know you're trying to get into debt and he'll help choose a special bottle or two. Finally, always treat those in your party.

Whether your pleasure is theater, concerts, nightclubs, or topless bars, a healthy diet of entertainment will help make you a better-rounded human being. Try opting for the front row or the VIP section (most of which have bar-tab minimums). Commissioned concierges or ticket agencies will find you the best seats *and* charge you a fee. If the evening in question comes up and you don't feel like going, put on your sweats and turn on the television—they're your tickets, so you don't have to go if you don't want to.

Fashion and Hygiene

The world of fashion includes clothing, accessories, and jewelry, all available in a staggering array of designers and high prices. As a debt embracer, you always want to look your best. "Clothes make the man," goes the old saying, and your sartorial presentation is the secret handshake to introduce you to other debtors. When in doubt, go designer. Not only will name-brand clothing and jewelry hold its value should you ever, heaven forbid, have to pawn it (see chapter 9, "Avoiding Payback: Bills, Collections, and Bankruptcy"), you never want to be without an answer to the question "I love your outfit—who's it by?" Last season's styles will never do for you; an important part of your *raison d'êbtre* is to reflect the best of the best *now*.

Your body serves as the canvas for your fashion sense, and to that end you never want to skimp on any kind of grooming. Haircuts and coloring,

---

Words Disbursed

"I like my money right where I can see it. Hanging in my closet."
— Sarah Jessica Parker, *Sex and the City*

---

full-body waxing, facials, manicures and pedicures—services like these are *necessities* for standard and acceptable personal upkeep. If you think you'll forget to schedule these appointments in a timely way, consider arranging a standing session every week or month.

Home Décor

Once you've got your dream house, the fun doesn't stop. Although you'll no doubt furnish the broad strokes early on, over time you need to buy the little touches that make a house a home. Objets d'art, bric-a-brac, tchotchkes, knickknacks, Fabergé eggs: you'd be surprised how quickly those can add up. When you see an end table that's infinitely better than the one you already own, buy it and get rid of the old one. You can never have enough bedding, towels, and throw blankets—preferable with high thread-counts and in sumptuous materials such as cashmere. And remember: you should *always* have fresh flowers.

Extravagance Role Model

After corrupt president Ferdinand Marcos and his family fled the Philippines for Hawaii, his wife, Imelda, was found to own 15 mink coats, 508 floor-length gowns, 888 handbags, 71 pairs of sunglasses, 65 parasols, 1 bullet-proof bra, 200 girdles, and over 1,060 pairs of shoes. Prior to the downfall, Imelda enjoyed $5 million shopping sprees in New York and Rome. In one interview, she stated, "I love beauty and I am allergic to ugliness. Beauty is God made real." Consistent with her spirituality, Imelda considered extravagance to be her duty to the poor. "You have to be some kind of light, a star to give them guidelines," she asserted. "The bigger we are as human beings the more greedy we become."

Vacations

Vacations constitute one of your debt rewards. It's hard work being you, and you deserve to get away from it all. If you choose to stay at a cheap motel with a lumpy mattress, how can that possibly help you escape your daily life? Instead, you'll want to cultivate the high life in both work and play.

There are few parts of a vacation that cannot be charged, from plane tickets to hotel rooms to gambling (an unparalleled way to accumulate debt). A few rules of thumb: dine in hotel restaurants or order room service, stay at a resort and charge everything to your room without looking at the bills, and ask hotel staff where to find the best shopping areas. At a minimum, you'll want to

take three vacations per year, plus a
handful of weekend getaways.

Daily, Unconscious Spending

You might be tempted to pooh-pooh your
small repetitive daily purchases. By virtue
of their repetition, however, they add up!
Daily, unconscious spending consists of the
expenditures you make throughout your
day without even registering them, such as
your two venti soy mochas (caffeinated in
the morning and decaf in the afternoon).
You don't feel the money come out of your
pocket because they don't cost a lot, but add
them up and they'll really make a contribu-
tion to your debt. Here's an example:

Venti Soy Mocha (VSM) = $5
2 VSMs / day = $10
$10 / day × 365 days = $3,650 per year

> **masstige:** From *mass* + pres*tige*. Prestige goods available at prices affordable to the masses, often with the imprimatur of a high-end designer or celebrity, such as Isaac Mizrahi's or Michael Graves's lines at Target.
>
> **maffluent:** From *mass* + a*ffluent*. Growing group of ordinary individuals who can claim affluence.

Try making other small purchases—lottery tickets, cigarettes, parking, a morning bagel and newspaper—a part of your daily routine.

The 24/7 World

Just because you get home late doesn't mean you don't have time to shop: the Internet is there for you 24 hours a day, 365 days a year. You can find anything your heart desires in the comfort of your home, wearing your pajamas. The Internet will keep a steady stream of packages arriving at your door—all paid by credit card. And if you spend enough time, energy, and money shopping online, or if you shop when you're tired or a little bit tipsy, you may even forget what you've ordered. What a nice surprise!

Dream Big

Spend, spend more, and then spend more than you thought you ever could. Use your creativity: rent out Yankee Stadium so your son can stand on the pitcher's mound. For your husband's company dinner, mix Versace and Prada. When you're at an art auction, raise your paddle. This is your time to dream big. You only live once, so don't hold back. Now that your credit acquisition and spending skills are top-notch, you're ready for the final stage of debt management: avoiding payback.

CHAPTER 9
AVOIDING PAYBACK:
BILLS, COLLECTIONS, AND BANKRUPTCY

SADLY, THERE COME MOMENTS IN
every debt embracer's life when envelopes
marked "DUE NOW" sail into the mailbox,
and it is to this disheartening phenomenon
that we will now take you. Payback is an
unnecessarily painful subject, and this
chapter will lead you through it without
panic or worry. The strategies and loopholes
at your disposal are plentiful, and knowing
them will qualify you as a truly skillful debt
embracer. In this chapter, we'll show you:

- Why a debt embracer pays on time.

- Why you'd rather be a "revolver" than
  a "deadbeat."

- How to play the shell game.

- How to plan your exit strategy.

Credit Card Bills

The savvy debt embracer must execute careful dance steps to insure both the minimum cash outflow and the maximum credit inflow. This involves knowing when to pay and how much, when to transfer a balance and to what card, and when and how to contact the credit card companies should trouble arise. While the debtor seeks to rack up mountains of debt as quickly as possible, credit must be managed for the long haul. If you make early, frequent, and amateurish mistakes, your credit will be shut down before your debt is out of the low five digits.

Pay the Minimum: No More, No Less

It is against the debt embracer's code of ethics to pay a monthly *credit* card bill in full, wasting precious cash and defeating the very definition of credit card. Financial institutions call customers who pay their complete balances every month "deadbeats." Instead, you want to be what these companies have christened a "revolver": someone who always carries a balance. As evidence of their preferred status, revolvers get the most credit card offers.

Always pay the minimum listed on your monthly bill. This paltry amount—around 2 or 3 percent of the total balance—is what your cash is for: leveraging maximum credit and, thus, debt.

Debt Budgets

In 1980, Americans spent one in nine of their take-home dollars paying off debt. In 2006, this statistic rose to one in seven! As a debt embracer, strive to keep that momentum going. Earmark at *least* one in four dollars of your household income to managing your debt. Reach for the stars!

Pay on Time

While utilities and other non-credit companies are forgiving when it comes to tardy payment, credit cards, mortgages, and other loan agencies can be inappropriately punitive. Because your goal is to keep your credit coming, do not try to change the system; instead, pay your bills on time. Penalties for tardy payment range from insignificant late fees to raised interest rates (which put more of your precious cash toward interest and less toward purchases) to badly dinged credit ratings (this is especially the case with mortgages), impairing your ability to get more credit.

With credit cards, paying late by a whole billing cycle—e.g., one month late—can trigger a "universal default" (UD). Though a UD can entail just one late bill, it will cause the interest rates on *all* your credit cards to go up at once. While this will speed your debt accumulation, you would rather spend this money on the things of your choice, not on interest.

The Shell Game

One use for all the credit card offers you receive in the mail is to pit them against one another. Say you have a credit card balance accumulating credit at 18.25 percent, and you receive an offer in the mail for a low introductory APR on balance transfers (anywhere from 0 to 9.99 percent). Open the new credit card account, then use it to pay off an old credit card balance, then continue making your minimum payments on the new card. Once the low APR expires, apply for another new credit card with a balance-transfer option. You can keep applying for new cards and rolling over your debt indefinitely. In effect, you are taking out new loans to pay off older loans under better terms.

Other Loans

Every once in a while, even the most ardent debt embracer will choose to consolidate all current debt in one place—such as a second mortgage or a HELOC—in order to start over with freshly minted credit cards. If you find your credit card debt getting unwieldy and inconvenient, seek other types of loans, as outlined in chapter 6.

Cash-Flow Problems

There comes a time in almost every debt embracer's life when cash becomes an issue. How do you know when this moment has come? When you have trouble paying your minimum payments on time, not because you've chosen to disregard your bills in the messy pile they've somehow accumulated but instead because you suspect or know that you lack enough cash on hand. Given your talents and punctual minimum payments, of course, you will have pushed this critical moment off as long as humanly

Cyber-Begging

Back at the turn of the last century, people who were deeply in debt wrote "begging letters" to famous wealthy people, pleading for a handout or a job. John D. Rockefeller and Andrew Carnegie received tens of thousands of letters every week. Now, you can harness the power of the Internet to raise cash. In 2002, a Brooklyn woman named Karyn Bosnak found herself $20,000 in credit card debt. With the realization that payoff would only take 20,000 people one dollar each, she posted a website asking for help—and paid off her debt in 20 weeks. Since then others have cyber-begged (also known as Internet panhandling) to raise money for getting out of bad marriages, plastic surgery, new cars, and gambling. All you need is a simple website linked to a PayPal account and you're in business.

possible. Before you move on to the next steps—collection agencies and bankruptcy—you will want to raise as much cash as possible without unduly compromising your lifestyle. Here are some options:

- **Increase your income.** While we haven't paid too much attention to the income side of the debt equation, there's no question that a higher income will allow you to support more debt for a longer period of time. Cash-flow difficulties can give you the shot of courage you need to go in to your boss and demand a raise. If your boss is unreasonable, interview for higher-paid positions. As a last resort, you can accept overtime work or find a second job, but this will seriously impede your pursuit of happiness.

- **Liquidate retirement accounts.** If you've ignored the anti-saving advice in chapter 4, now's the time to cash in. Ignore the advisor's warnings about early-withdrawal penalties and so forth—you need cash!

- **Pawn or auction off your belongings.** As outlined in chapter 8, one of the advantages of buying high-quality designer items is they hold their value. Pawnbrokers will give you about one-third of the item's resale value in cash. They agree to hold it for a specified period, and if you return within that time frame to buy the item back, it's yours; otherwise, the pawnbroker will sell it. Online auction services such as eBay can also be a lucrative way to raise money from belongings. All you need to do is take digital pictures of items for sale, post them, and watch the money roll in.

- **Sell your car or house.** While these last-case scenarios may not be worthwhile because you have little or no equity invested, they are worth exploring when other options have been exhausted.

And if you think repossession is likely, it's always better to sell beforehand.

Collection Agencies

When creditors determine that accounts are not being paid, they usually delegate the process to an outside collection agency. The agency either works on a commission basis to collect the money for the creditor or buys the bad debt (for a percentage of the debt's face value) from the creditor and attempts to collect it on its own behalf.

Fortunately, most debt collectors work on commission, so they're not motivated to break your legs. And, as an American consumer, you have legal rights. The Fair Debt Collections Practices Act prohibits bullying tactics and gives consumers the right to sue should these rules be infringed.

Know Your Rights

Don't let collection agencies intimidate you. You have grounds for a lawsuit if they do any of the following:

- Tell your boss, neighbors, or friends that you're in debt.
- Contact you if you've notified them that you have a lawyer.
- Call you before 8 AM or after 9 PM.
- Call you at work if your employer disapproves of such contact.
- Use profanity or threats of violence.
- Harass, oppress, or abuse you.
- Falsely imply that they are attorneys or government representatives or work for a credit bureau.
- Falsely imply that you have committed a crime, that you will be arrested, or that they can seize your possessions or garnish your wages.
- Give inaccurate information to credit-reporting agencies.
- Illegally take or threaten to take a debtor's assets, bank accounts, or paycheck.
- Contact you by postcard.

If any of this occurs, call your state's attorney general and the Federal Trade Commission (FTC) to turn the tables on the bully.

To avoid collection agencies, you'll want to screen your calls with an answering machine. You can call the phone company to block the collector's phone number, or change your phone number. If you get a letter from a collection agency, seal it and send it back with a "No longer at this address" note. Finally, you are legally entitled to send a "Cease Communication" letter stating that "Under section 805-C of the Fair Debt Collection Practices Act, I request that you cease further communication with me." Be sure to send this letter with return receipt.

Credit Counseling

While many debt embracers will choose direct bankruptcy to erase their debts, some opt for an intermediary step, credit counseling—and, since the Bankruptcy

Abuse Prevention and Consumer Protection Act (BAPCA) of 2005 was implemented, credit counseling is mandatory for those who seek to file bankruptcy.

To utilize this resource, debtors contact a nonprofit counseling agency. A counselor works with the debtor to create a debt management plan (DMP), which generally entails the closure of current accounts, agreements with creditors to accept decreased payback and interest rates, and consolidation of debts into one monthly payment. The counselor will also help with personal budgeting.

The credit-counseling industry has been the target of consumer and government complaints, in part because many are paid by creditors (especially credit card companies) in the hopes that bankruptcy, and therefore lack of payback, will be averted. In 2003, the Federal Trade Commission, IRS, and many state regulators issued a consumer alert about tax-exempt credit-counseling organizations, recommending that individuals seeking counseling should exercise caution when selecting an agency. In particular, the report warned against credit counselors demanding high fees and touting a quick fix or any guarantees. Be sure to look up any prospective counselor with the appropriate state agency and the Better Business Bureau.

Bankruptcy

Sadly, the Bankruptcy Abuse Prevention and Consumer Protection Act (BAPCA) of 2005 ended the golden era of bankruptcy for American debt embracers. On the eve of the new law, bankruptcy filings hit record

Famously Bankrupt

Many notable individuals have embraced debt with enough fervor to ferry them along to bankruptcy. What stellar company you keep!

- P. T. Barnum
- Kim Basinger
- L. Frank Baum
- Robert Blake
- Lorraine Bracco
- Dorothy Dandridge
- Dino De Laurentiis
- Walt Disney
- Ulysses S. Grant
- Tony Gwynn
- MC Hammer
- Larry King
- Abraham Lincoln
- Willie Nelson
- Burt Reynolds
- Debbie Reynolds
- Donald Trump
- Mark Twain
- Mike Tyson
- Oscar Wilde

numbers, increasing almost 40 percent over the same period in the preceding year, as debtors rushed to avail themselves of the old rules.

However, as you learned in chapter 3, people used to go to debtors prison—and worse—for failing to pay their debts. In the United States, the Constitution gives Congress the right to govern bankruptcy; the current bankruptcy law (with amendments) is the Bankruptcy Act of 1978. Despite BAPCA, bankruptcy is still an accepted exit strategy for debt.

Bankruptcy is the legal declaration that you are unable to pay your debts. Once you file for bankruptcy, the process is designed to liquidate and rehabilitate your estate as well as protect you from creditors. In the United States, the decision to declare bankruptcy is a voluntary one.

Bankruptcy once carried a stigma. In some lists, it was included among the top five negative life events, along with divorce, severe illness, disability, and death of a loved one. Now, however, people throw bankruptcy parties! This change in perspective is borne out by the numbers: according to the American Bankruptcy Institute (the "Essential Resource for Today's Busy Insolvency Professional"), the number of consumer-filed bankruptcies has risen from 287,564 in 1980 to 2,039,214 in 2005, up from 80 percent of total filings (versus business) to almost 94 percent! That means 1 out of 100 adults in the United States declare bankruptcy—an exclusive but by no means fringe club.

Personal bankruptcy falls into two types, Chapter 7 (Liquidation) and Chapter 13 (Reorganization). BAPCA made the requirements for Chapter 7, which erases debt, more stringent, so most people will qualify only for Chapter 13, which requires slow repayment of debt over three to five years at a rate not to exceed 25 percent of your monthly income.

If you do decide to file for bankruptcy, there's light at the end of the tunnel: while the bankruptcy will stay on your credit report for seven to ten years, a study by the Credit Research Center at Purdue University found that one-third of consumers who had filed for bankruptcy had obtained credit within three years of filing, and one-half within five years. Soon you'll be able to start accumulating debt once again, and your total lifetime debt achievement becomes the amount eliminated in bankruptcy *plus* your new debt.

What a Ride!

Congratulations, debt embracer—you've racked up mountains of debt and, if necessary, you've found the best exit strategy for you. Whether you've chosen to motor at country lane or autobahn speeds, it's been an exhilarating run. Hopefully you have all kinds of glittery, sumptuous personal belongings and vacation-of-a-lifetime memories to show for your efforts.

CHAPTER 10
CONCLUSION:
TAKING DEBT TO THE NEXT LEVEL

NOW THAT YOU'VE LEARNED WHY
and how to grow your financial debt, you're
ready to explore alternative debt curren-
cies: moral, intellectual, interpersonal,
and oxygen. You first started this journey
thinking the rewards would be exclusively
financial, but debt is so much more. When
you consider that debt consists merely of
using more resources than you contribute,
the debt mentality can translate into every
arena. Further, each of the nonfinancial
debt arenas can lead to corresponding forms
of bankruptcy—and as an added bonus,
moral, intellectual, and interpersonal bankruptcy are not regulated by the government.

Moral Debt

There are a number of definitions and usages for moral debt. Moral debt plays a role in Christian theology, wherein human sins created a moral debt that God paid for with the sacrifice of his son, Jesus Christ. In beliefs around karma and reincarnation, moral debts—the consequences of past actions—carry through successive incarnations until they are repaid. In secular terms, moral debt is posited between the generations; the living are beholden to the hard work and sacrifices of the preceding generations as well as to ensuring the quality of life of future generations. Moral debt is sometimes discussed in reference to the social contract, the unspoken fabric that keeps fellow citizens (for the most part) from harming each other. In foreign policy, one can speak of a nation's moral debt for previous bad actions, as with Germany toward the Jews. Finally, moral debt enters socioeconomics with the idea that the wealthy owe a moral debt to the poor.

In racking up your own moral debt, you can think about treating people badly and using more than your fair share of resources. For example, if you cut someone off when you're driving, you've just increased your moral debt a little bit. If you fail to recycle and own a gas-guzzling car, you've taken out moral debt from future generations. In general, anything bad that you do can be construed as contributing to your moral debt.

Intellectual Debt

When you borrow somebody's ideas, whether friend or published author, you extend yourself into intellectual debt. The intellectual debt deepens if you don't cite the source in question or if you fail over a lifetime to contribute any original ideas to the knowledge marketplace.

On a small scale, this could encompass telling a great joke without acknowledging where you first heard it—or by saying that you yourself made it up. On a larger scale, this can entail outright plagiarism.

Interpersonal Debt

Interpersonal debt trades in the currency of favors. Whether you rely on family, friends, or coworkers, if someone does you a favor, you begin to accumulate interpersonal debt.

To grow your interpersonal debt, ask people to do things for you—a back rub, some house-sitting, helping out with a report. When they later ask *you* for help, refuse. Of course, you'll want to come up with good excuses so that your interpersonal creditors don't stifle your ongoing credit.

Oxygen Debt

Oxygen debt occurs during intense exercise when the lungs cannot provide enough oxygen to meet the muscles' requirements. Because the muscles do not have sufficient oxygen for aerobic respiration, they shift into anaerobic respiration, breaking down glucose for short-term energy. This glucose breakdown produces lactic acid, causing the sensation of fatigue as well as potential cramping. When the body returns to rest, it must repay the oxygen debt, using more oxygen to break down the accumulated lactic acid than would be required for the normal breakdown of glucose. Oxygen debts are generally repaid through panting.

The Facile Debtor

As a committed debtor, you are what you drive. You spend more than you earn and take more than you give. Your goal is to get something for nothing, and you believe strongly in the free lunch. And now that you've finished *How to Get into Debt*, you've certainly earned that lunch. Bon appétit.

Words Disbursed
"Blessed are the young, for they shall inherit the national debt." —Herbert Hoover